QUESTIONS IN HISTORY

Series editor: Alan White

MUSSOLINI IN POWER

Martyn Whittock

Collins Educational

To John Worth, a good friend to me and to justice and freedom.

Printed by Collins Educational
An imprint of HarperCollins*Publishers* Ltd
77–85 Fulham Palace Road
London W6 8JB

© HarperCollins*Publishers* Ltd

First published 1998
Reprinted 1999

ISBN 0 00 327122 6

British Library Cataloguing in Publication Data
A catalogue record for this book is available from the British Library.

Acknowledgements

I would like to thank a number of people who assisted me in the writing of this book. Steve Tamplin of Queen Elizabeth's School, Wimborne commented critically on the text, as did Boyd Gray at Kingdown School, Warminster. My Lower Sixth students Amy, Rhiannon, Madaleine, Becky, Alex, Matthew, James and Simon also assisted me with comments.

The author and publishers would like to thank the following for permission to reproduce illustrations:

Imperial War Museum (p23)

Cover photograph: Photo AKG London / Elsbeth Heddenhausen

Edited by Lucy Courtenay
Designed by Derek Lee
Map by Tony Richardson
Production by Anna Pauletti

Printed and bound by Scotprint Musselburgh

Contents

1 The roots of dictatorship 1922–25

How and when was Mussolini able to convert government into dictatorship?

Key points

- ◆ From which point should we date Mussolini in power?
- ◆ How and when did Mussolini move from constitutional rule to dictatorship?
- ◆ What implications did this have for the later character of Fascist rule?

In office but not in power?

From what point should we date Mussolini's control of the Italian state? The start-date for Mussolini's government is 1922. In this year, although Fascists claimed that their March on Rome was a kind of Fascist revolution, Mussolini was in reality legally and constitutionally appointed as Prime Minister by King Victor Emmanuel III. Yet the appointment of Mussolini as Prime Minister on 30 October 1922 did not in fact bring the kind of power desired by him and the Fascist *squadristi* who had paved the way to this event.

- ◆ Mussolini lacked a Fascist majority in parliament.

- ◆ The king had the support of the military and could dismiss Mussolini.

- ◆ Mussolini was forced to rely on a working relationship with the Liberals and Popolari. These were democratic political parties, the Popolari being a Catholic party. This coalition reassured the parties of the Right who felt that the system was not threatened by Mussolini, given the divided nature of Fascism with its lack of a united philosophy and structure.

Mussolini did not march on Rome, but made his way there by train. Or, as Denis Mack Smith has put it, Mussolini did not seize control of the state in 1922 but took a 'sleeping car to power'. Mack Smith implies that this was symbolic of the fact that he gained power through an orderly and constitutional transition, not a Fascist revolution.

Mussolini himself was well aware that 1922 had not given him a secure grip on power and he was careful to keep up the momentum:

- ◆ As well as holding the post of Prime Minister, Mussolini ensured that he held the posts of Minister of the Interior and Minister of Foreign Affairs.

- ◆ He maintained the threat of Fascist violence, which kept other parties in a state of alarm and made it difficult for them to oppose the one man who seemed able to keep a rein on that violence.

◆ He played on the fear of the Left which paralysed the middle classes and industrialists. The so-called threat from the Left became a justification for his need of special powers, and excused any 'temporary measures' which went against the spirit of democracy.

How and when did Mussolini move from constitutional rule to dictatorship?

In 1922 Mussolini sought approval for exercising emergency powers over a period of twelve months. He was careful to stress that this was only necessary in order to diffuse Fascist violence and to benefit Italy. These features are clear in a speech Mussolini delivered to the Italian parliament:

> 'I could have made a bivouac of this gloomy hall; I could have shut up parliament and formed a government only of Fascists. I could have done this but I did not wish to do so, any rate at the moment ... I have formed a coalition government, not with the intention of obtaining a parliamentary majority, with which at the moment I can perfectly well dispense, but in order to gather in support of the suffering nation all those who, over and above questions of party and section, wish to save her ... Before arriving here we were asked on all sides for a programme. It is not, alas, programmes that are wanting in Italy but men to carry them out.'

The response of parliament was to give him a massive vote of confidence and the grant of emergency powers. Although Communists and Socialists opposed him, the Liberals supported him, regarding him as a decisive ruler who was necessary for the peace and security of Italy.

In 1923 Mussolini secured the support of the Confindustria, the pressure group representing Italian industrialists. It was a support gained by Mussolini dropping plans to pursue tax evaders and toning down the more radical demands that had once characterised Fascism. In similar fashion, Mussolini – once a vehement critic of the Catholic Church – confirmed government intentions to ban contraceptives and to support compulsory religious education in state schools. This friendly gesture was met by a return gesture from the Vatican, who withdrew support from the Catholic Popolari party in 1923.

A clever combination of intimidation and fear of the Left helped secure the passage of the Acerbo Law in July 1923. This replaced the old electoral system, in which a number of parties had political influence, with a system by which any party which polled more than 25% of the total votes cast and was the largest single party would take two-thirds of the parliamentary seats. At one stroke it seemed to offer a way out of indecisive minority governments and shifting coalition parties. There was now the promise of strong and stable government. From Mussolini's point of view, it offered the kind of parliamentary majority which would allow him to convert his temporary powers into a permanent dictatorship. In April 1924 the Fascists and their allies gained 66% of the vote and secured total control of the parliamentary system.

The death of Matteotti

Not every opposition politician was overawed by Fascist threats. One such politician was the Socialist Giacomo Matteotti. He accused the Fascists of using violence and intimidation during the election campaign of 1924. On 10

June 1924, Matteotti was kidnapped by a Fascist gang and stabbed to death. The event shocked many who had been prepared to cooperate with Mussolini.

In protest at the killing, Socialist and Communist deputies refused to attend meetings of the Italian parliament. They were supported by some members of the Popolari who disapproved of the support given to Mussolini by the leadership of their party. This move – called the Aventine Secession after an event in ancient Roman history when the poorer people of Rome had briefly withdrawn from the city to force concessions from their rulers – was meant to isolate Mussolini and to expose the lack of support for the Fascists. However, it did not succeed for two main reasons:

◆ The king refused to dismiss Mussolini, fearing that this would mean the triumph of the Left and possibly civil war.

◆ Some Liberals and conservatives such as Giovanni Giolitti and Antonio Salandra continued to support Mussolini, fearing that there was no alternative and hoping to have more influence over a weak Prime Minister.

The move to dictatorship

Faced with this crisis, Mussolini moved to weaken the opposition by introducing press censorship in July 1924 and banning meetings of opposition parties. The parties themselves were finally banned in December 1925. But the move to a seizure of power was not simply calculated by Mussolini to draw advantage from a crisis. He was being driven to act by radical Fascists. Mussolini found himself caught between a mounting opposition and discontented Fascists who wanted the establishment of a real dictatorship. In November 1924, the ranks of the opposition were swollen by the addition of Mussolini's Liberal allies, who realised they could not control or influence Mussolini after all.

The indecisiveness of Mussolini in the face of this is striking. In December, leading Fascists demanded that Mussolini act to end the crisis and turn his government into a dictatorship. This brought to a head the conflict between those in the Fascist Party who wanted extremist government and those who desired a legal transition to the eventual Fascist state, whatever that might be.

On 3 January 1925 Mussolini made the decisive move. He accepted full responsibility for all Fascist action up to that date and stated that 'Italy wants peace and quiet, and to get on with its work. I shall give it all these, if possible in love, but if necessary by force.'

Backed by a parliamentary majority and allowed freedom of action by the king's own inaction, Mussolini set about finally constructing the dictatorship he had been moving towards since 1922. In January he set up a committee to reform the constitution. By the end of 1925 he had banned all opposition parties and trade unions, established a secret police and a special court to try political crimes and replaced elected mayors by Fascist officials. All of these acts were embodied in a law passed in December 1925. Additionally, Mussolini was made responsible not to the chamber of deputies but directly to the king. Combined with press censorship, curtailment of meetings, and rule by decree (from January 1926), these acts ensured that Mussolini was now firmly in control of the Italian state.

How and why was Mussolini successful, 1922–25?

◆ An exaggerated fear of the Left paralysed Liberal and conservative politicians. It was a fear played upon by Mussolini. But it was based on real instability in Italian society, which was turbulent and fractured in the aftermath of the First World War.

◆ Right-wing politicians and industrialists were concerned with their own self-interest, such as defeating trade unions and crushing the Left.

◆ The king lacked the will to remove Mussolini.

◆ Liberals and conservatives underestimated Mussolini, thinking they could manipulate him during the Matteotti crisis.

◆ The opposition were hopelessly split and could not unite to block the Fascists.

◆ The radical Fascists forced Mussolini into more radical action.

◆ There was genuine popular support for Mussolini.

What implications did this have for the character of later Fascist rule?

What is clear from all this is that, in many ways, Mussolini's taking of power should be dated more to 1925 than to 1922. Yet the establishment of the dictatorship in 1925 (developed by further expansion of his power in 1926) would not have been possible without the events of 1922. Furthermore, the years between 1922 and 1925 had seen both the steady erosion of democracy and the growth of personal dictatorship, which together were to act as a launch pad for the dramatic events of 1925. This process of a drift to dictatorship between 1922 and 1925 was to have three profound effects on the character of the eventual Fascist dictatorship.

The traditional approach

First, the dictatorship was less of a break with the past and more an acceleration of trends within Italian politics. In the 19th century, the Italian Risorgimento (the movement which had led to a united Italy) had harnessed forces that were not as liberal and democratic as are sometimes presented. Indeed, 'a patriotic movement like the Risorgimento can easily lead by its own logic to nationalism and imperialism' (D. Mack Smith, quoted in *Modern History Review*, 1990). The struggles for a united Italy in the 19th century had encouraged a pride in Italian culture and achievements, but had also increased the power of the traditional Italian ruling classes and prompted a sense of frustration that Italy was still a weak state. This meant than many people in Italian government and society could recognise traditional features in Mussolini's nationalist aims and ambitions.

No real break with the past

Since the late 19th century, Italy had been dominated by a small class of rich and powerful people who had little in common with ordinary Italians. Mussolini was able to achieve such huge success because the political parties of the late 19th and early 20th centuries had failed to bridge the gap between the rich and the poor. Ordinary Italians were made to feel important by Mussolini's propaganda and came to support him. Their previous lack of involvement in the so-called 'liberal state' meant that Mussolini's aloof and domineering government was surprisingly acceptable to many who had once worked within democracy. Ordinary Italians found it easier to work within Fascist Italy than might have been expected. Furthermore, the old Italian state had often used its own prefects to manipulate politics in the regions.

Radical pressure

Thirdly, it was the force of the radical Fascist *squadristi* which 'not only transformed Fascism from an impotent grouping to a powerful paramilitary movement but eventually forced Mussolini's hand by making further compromise with liberalism impossible' (R. Griffin, *The Nature of Fascism*, 1991). This was a feature that was forgotten by neither Mussolini nor the radical Fascists in the years after 1925. For Mussolini, it was a memory which led him to attempt to break free from the constraints of party control. For the *squadristi*, it was a memory which encouraged them to put more pressure on Mussolini at key points in the history of his administration.

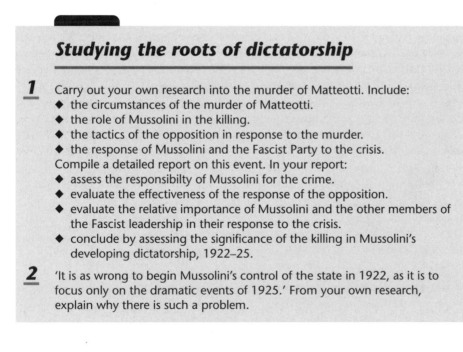

Studying the roots of dictatorship

1   Carry out your own research into the murder of Matteotti. Include:
- the circumstances of the murder of Matteotti.
- the role of Mussolini in the killing.
- the tactics of the opposition in response to the murder.
- the response of Mussolini and the Fascist Party to the crisis.

Compile a detailed report on this event. In your report:
- assess the responsibilty of Mussolini for the crime.
- evaluate the effectiveness of the response of the opposition.
- evaluate the relative importance of Mussolini and the other members of the Fascist leadership in their response to the crisis.
- conclude by assessing the significance of the killing in Mussolini's developing dictatorship, 1922–25.

2   'It is as wrong to begin Mussolini's control of the state in 1922, as it is to focus only on the dramatic events of 1925.' From your own research, explain why there is such a problem.

2 Was Mussolini a strong or weak dictator?

The nature of Fascist government and the extent of Mussolini's power

---

Key points

◆ What style of leadership is suggested by the appearance of Mussolini's government after 1926?
◆ What was the reality of Mussolini in power?
◆ What was the relationship between Fascism and the old elites?
◆ How was opposition treated?
◆ Mussolini – a weak dictator?

What style of leadership is suggested by Mussolini's government after 1926?

After 1926, Mussolini gives the appearance of being very much in control of Fascist government in Italy. In December 1925 he had instituted the new position of Head of Government. In this role, Mussolini was responsible not to parliament but to the king, who alone had power to dismiss him. By freeing himself from parliament, Mussolini had freed himself from the constraints of democracy and had opened up the route to personal dictatorship. From January 1926 Mussolini had the power to make laws by decree instead of going through even the semblance of parliamentary rule. It was a power he made the most of. By the time he fell from power in 1943, he had issued over 100,000 such decrees. Parliamentary government had effectively ended.

As well as being the focus of state power, Mussolini was free from the irritation of criticism by any effective opposition:

◆ The Liberals and Popolari were divided and lacked leadership.

◆ The socialists and communists were subject to physical attack and were scattered.

◆ The king lacked the will to stand up to Mussolini.

Indeed, in 1928 even the power of the monarchy to influence government was reduced when the king lost the power to appoint the Prime Minister. Instead, the Fascist Grand Council drew up a list of candidates for him to choose from.

All these actions suggest that after 1926, Mussolini took large steps towards the establishment of a personal dictatorship centred on his possession of absolute power. It was this position of power that became encapsulated in the Italian title 'il Duce', the new Caesar. The government controlled the press and manipulated the images Italians had of their leader and government. Any positive foreign assessments were trumpeted, and Mussolini was presented as the hard-working, athletic, brilliant and all-knowing ruler. Slogans such as 'Mussolini is always right' and 'Believe, Obey, Fight' became commonplace, and all demanded unquestioning obedience to the benevolent but ruthless Duce. Coupled with this was the presentation of ideas in easily accessible forms, accompanied by public spectacles.

In appearance, at least, Mussolini had created an overarching dictatorship, which intervened in all aspects of the lives of Italian people and accepted only total loyalty. As he expressed it himself in the *Enciclopedia Italiana* in 1931, 'The Fascist conception of the state is all-embracing and outside of the state no human or spiritual values can exist, let alone be desirable'. Earlier, in June 1925, Mussolini had described his own view of his dictatorship, claiming he represented a 'ferocious totalitarian will'. This claim implied that he totally dominated the Italian state. However, was he really as powerful as he claimed to be? Did his totalitarian state really exist?

What was the reality of Mussolini in power?

Mussolini's first battle for supreme leadership was fought with his own Fascist Party (the PNF). In January 1923 he disbanded the Fascist squads and recruited their members into a Militia (MVSN) controlled by the state. However, the *squadristi* were not so easily tamed. In the spring of 1925, the radical PNF secretary Roberto Farinacci launched what nearly became a 'revolution from below'. Encouraging the wild and destructive personalities so common amongst the ordinary Fascist members – the *squadristi* – Farinacci ignored the Interior Minister Luigi Federzoni's instructions that only state organs should control law and order. This violence encouraged those Fascists who felt that Mussolini was already betraying his radical roots and had abandoned a 'Fascist Revolution'.

This state of violent unrest ended in October 1925 following a rampage through Florence by out-of-control *squadristi*. Mussolini had no intention of being dominated by the PNF and its radicals. With the backing of the Fascist Grand Council he banned the squads, purged the Fascist organisation in Florence, and in March 1926 replaced the radical Farinacci with the more compliant Filippo Turati.

Turati went on to restructure the local party organisations, making them more subservient to the central organisation of the PNF and to Mussolini. Already in 1923 Mussolini had conducted a purge of the PNF, removing people who did not accept his authority. This was followed in 1928 by a further purge, which removed over 60,000 PNF members and broke the influence of radicals such as Farinacci within the Fascist Party. From this date onwards all provincial party posts would be decided in Rome. The PNF radicals had been 'replaced or domesticated' (P. Morgan, *Italian Fascism*, 1995).

How was Mussolini able to dominate the PNF?

Mussolini was successful in his domination of the PNF for a number of reasons:

◆ The PNF had no clear ideology, character or philosophy (see Chapter 3).

◆ The PNF was a complex alliance of factions, often holding conflicting beliefs. The unifying force was Mussolini, and the factions jockeyed for position around him and tried to gain his favour.

◆ Mussolini skilfully manipulated these divisions and rivalries.

◆ Mussolini promoted the compliant rather than the independent thinkers, and men such as Italo Balbo and Dino Grandi found themselves sidelined.

◆ After 1931, the PNF expanded its membership and the old core of *squadristi* found themselves swamped. The old party had been dominated by workers and peasants. The new party was dominated by the white-collar class, who saw membership of the PNF as a useful tool in their career plans.

In these ways the PNF, which had launched Mussolini to power, found it had been used and discarded. The PNF became just one amongst many interest groups in Fascist Italy such as the Catholic Church, the government, the civil service and the industrialists.

Mussolini and government

Mussolini dominated the Fascist Party and set out to dominate government too. In this he was far less successful. He deliberately prevented other leading members of the government from meeting together to discuss policies. Instead they met Mussolini separately and remained divided and dominated by him. As part of this concentration of power he took over the key ministries himself. By 1929, Mussolini held eight ministries including Foreign Affairs, the Interior and Defence. 'Government came to resemble Mussolini in endless dialogue with himself' (P. Morgan, *Italian Fascism*, 1995). However, the image of power was an illusion. Mussolini simply could not monitor his own decisions across so many areas of government. He was often ignored and made little effort to investigate how his decisions were implemented.

Just as Mussolini had freed himself from the PNF, so he soon moved to free himself from parliamentary control. Even though it was dominated by Fascist deputies, parliament lost the right to debate and criticise policy. From May 1928 the system of government became established as a Senate, comprised of people appointed for life by the king, and a Chamber of Deputies made up of 400 deputies chosen by the Fascist Grand Council from a list of 1000 names put forward by the various Fascist-dominated organisations. The final list of 400 deputies was voted for in a plebiscite. This meant that all deputies were approved by the Fascist Party. Results in the eventual elections often ran at 98% in favour of the official government list. In 1928 the Fascist Grand Council officially became part of the Italian state. Eventually, in 1939, the parliament was abolished and replaced by a Chamber of Fasces and Corporations, select-ed from the Fascist syndicates (see Chapter 4).

Local self-government was abolished and replaced by appointed officials known as Provincial Prefects. There was a great deal of rivalry between the local PNF leadership and these Provincial Prefects. It was a rivalry decided in favour of the Prefects. This was because the Prefects enhanced the power of central government and so of Mussolini. In 1927 Mussolini declared that the local Fascists 'must collaborate in a subordinate role' with the Prefects. This division and competition was seen throughout Italian society – the civil service competed with the Fascist corporations and syndicates, the army competed with the Fascist militia. These rivalries and divisions increased Mussolini's personal power but made Fascist government chaotic and inefficient.

What was the relationship between Fascism and the old elites?

Mussolini never destroyed or replaced the old Italian elites – those groups in Italian society who had the greatest power and influence. The continued existence of these elites reduced the amount of real power held by Mussolini. In 1927 for instance, only about 15% of the civil service were members of the PNF. Even when this figure increased dramatically in the 1930s, it did not mean that the new members were sincere Fascists, but rather that they had recognised the usefulness of PNF membership.

For a long time this did not appear to matter. The elites were either satisfied with Mussolini's rule or grudgingly accepted it. Even the king, though he did not like Mussolini, made no attempt to control him. In this Mussolini was encouraged by the traditional position of the Italian monarchy, which had always distanced itself from the domestic affairs of Italian governments. But as problems grew in the late 1930s and especially during the Second World War, Mussolini's failure to control these elite groups was to lead to his downfall. However, for much of the period 1922–40, Mussolini defused any potential opposition.

Mussolini and the Catholic Church

One of the triumphs of Mussolini was establishing a working relationship with the Catholic Church. It was a success that had eluded every other Italian government since 1871. To do this, Mussolini abandoned the anti-Christian propaganda that had been a feature of Fascism prior to 1922. In 1929 this was rewarded by the Lateran Pacts:

◆ In the Lateran Treaty, the Pope recognised the existence of the Italian state and its authority over Rome and other land that had once been ruled by the Pope. In return, the Fascist state recognised the right of the Pope to rule in the Vatican City. Under Article 43 of the Treaty, Mussolini promised non-interference with the youth organisation Catholic Action.

◆ In an agreement called the Concordat, Catholicism was recognised as the state religion, the Pope could appoint bishops (the state reserved the right to refuse any it did not like) and the state paid the salary of clergy. Religious education became compulsory in schools, and there could be no divorce without Church consent.

◆ In a third agreement the Catholic Church was paid £30 million compensation for lost land and property.

Mussolini gained a great deal of prestige from these agreements, which also bound Catholics closer to the Fascist regime. They 'could not conspire against a regime constantly backed by the blessings of the Church' (G. Miccoli, 1973). For the Catholic Church the arrangements, in the words of Pope Pius XI, 'brought God to Italy and Italy to God'. The agreements promised to open the way for the Church to gain greater influence in the state. In the same way Mussolini hoped to gain greater influence in the life of Catholics.

The international scene in the 1930s encouraged many Italian Catholics to view Fascism as a protective barrier against worse ideologies. They hoped it would prevent the spread of both Nazism and communism. Significant numbers within the Catholic Church supported Mussolini's actions in Abyssinia, the Spanish Civil War and the invasion of the USSR in 1941.

Nevertheless, by the late 1930s the relationship was in trouble. Although Mussolini had exempted the youth organisation Catholic Action from the ban on all non-Fascist youth groups as part of the Lateran Treaty, the government had attempted to suppress it as early as 1931. The Church resisted Mussolini's action, and by promising that Catholic Action would limit itself to Church activities, persuaded him to back off. The result was that a large organisation involving many thousands of young people remained beyond the reach of the government. This came to have an increasingly important influence.

There had always been a complex relationship between Fascism and the Catholic Church. Some clergy supported Mussolini's anti-communism and promotion of family life, whilst others were utterly repelled by his fundamental anti-Christian beliefs and his later racism. Research has shown that amongst these latter clergy, there were real attempts to establish a Christian approach to politics which was independent of both Fascism and Liberalism.

In 1938 the Pope condemned Mussolini's anti-Semitic legislation, and by 1939 the relationship between Church and Fascism was in crisis. During the war, the Church was to become one of the centres of opposition to the regime, though not involved in outright rebellion.

The military, the police and the civil service

There was always friction between the army and the more ambitious *squadristi*. It was a rivalry largely decided in favour of the army, despite the continued existence of the Fascist militia. The military hierarchy were at last won over by the expansionist foreign policy of the 1930s and by promotions lavishly poured on its senior ranks.

The police remained a career service, not an extension of the Fascist party. Bocchini, a civil servant, remained the Chief of Police between 1926 and 1940. The police, like the army, was never brought under PNF control, and the Fascist militia 'Investigation Units' never developed into a party political police force in the way that the Nazi SD developed in Germany.

Similarly, the civil service remained unpurged. In spite of this it became remarkably loyal, won over by the benefits gained from supporting the regime. In the 1930s many civil servants were among the large numbers of white-collar workers who joined the PNF.

The one area which did experience something like a purge was the judiciary. Here Mussolini removed a great many judges who were not in sympathy with his political aims. He also interfered in the judicial process to ensure that sentences were to his liking.

How was opposition treated?

The Decree of Public Security (1926) put under police control and surveillance 'whoever are singled out by public rumour as being dangerous to the national order of the state'. The Fascists had already shown their attitude towards opponents in the years before 1926. Trade union offices and socialist and communist organisations had been attacked. The forced consumption of live toads and castor oil in early Fascism is legendary, but a more serious reminder lies in the murder of Matteotti in 1924.

Once he was in full power, Mussolini made this attitude towards opposition a permanent state. The Law for the Defence of the State (also in 1926) set up a Special Tribunal which swiftly processed anyone accused of political crimes. Verdicts for crimes such as these were politically motivated, and many other people were imprisoned without even this attempt to imitate justice. At this time, penal colonies were established on the islands of Lipari and Lampedusa.

A secret police force (OVRA) harried opposition. The only organised groups that managed to survive, in an underground existence, were the communists and a small Liberal-Socialist alliance organised by Carlo Roselli. Socialist and Catholic trade unions and strikes were banned by the Vidoni Palace Pact of 1925 which won Mussolini the support of the industrialists at the expense of the workers, whose freedoms were reduced.

Repression was an essential part of the Mussolini dictatorship. Nevertheless, it never assumed the character that it did in Nazi Germany. Violence was always present but in a more restrained form. Internal exile was used for many dissidents and there were probably fewer than 5000 political prisoners. For many people keeping quiet meant safety, and so they did not challenge the government. In addition, there was a great deal of support for Mussolini until the late 1930s, meaning that, for many, repression was not needed to ensure their compliance with the regime.

Mussolini – a weak dictator?

On one hand, Mussolini was in a very powerful position after 1926:

◆ He personally dominated both the PNF and the Italian government.

◆ The old Liberal structure of government was thoroughly reorganised and brought under Fascist control, which meant under the control of the Duce.

◆ His careful handling of the elites meant that they did not pose a serious threat to his power.

◆ His understanding with the Vatican removed a source of deep friction which had beset Italian society for over fifty years – something which no other Italian government had been able to achieve.

◆ The manipulation of the courts and the presence of the OVRA meant that opposition was virtually impossible. Those who attempted to oppose Mussolini were caught between repression and the genuine enthusiasm felt for the Duce until the later 1930s.

On the other hand, things were not really what they seemed:

◆ Mussolini's control over government was counterproductive. He had power but lacked the ability and energy to see decisions through, and often the day-to-day running of major government departments went on with little regard to him.

◆ The support for Mussolini from the elites of Church, civil service, military and police should not be confused with his having total control over them. Rather, Mussolini and the elites had an alliance of interests, which gave Mussolini considerable freedom of action while it lasted. However, had this delicate balance been disrupted, the shallow roots of Mussolini's dominance would soon have been exposed. By the late 1930s, the alliance dominance would soon have been exposed. By the late 1930s, the alliance was already coming under strain. The war was to accelerate this process.

◆ In the same way, the lack of opposition arose from the genuine support felt for Mussolini, but this too could and would be shaken by any inability on his part to satisfy the huge expectations he had raised.

As with so much in Fascist Italy, the appearance should not be confused with the underlying reality. The 'all-seeing' and 'energetic' Duce, who lived only for his country, was actually fast asleep while the lights in his study burned deep into the night as a public display of his ferocious will. The apparent power of the dictator rested on the appearance of control, a sham from which Mussolini would be rudely awoken when disappointment and disaster revealed the inadequacies of his philosophy and his personal rule.

Studying the nature of Mussolini's government

1 From what you have read in this chapter (and other research) construct a table:

Evidence for Mussolini as strong ruler	Evidence for Mussolini as weak ruler
Historical interpretations which support this view.	Historical interpretations which support this view.

Using this table as a writing frame, answer the following question:

2 'Mussolini's power lay more in appearance than substance'. Discuss. In your answer:
   ◆ Explain the issues and problems that need to be addressed.
   ◆ Critically examine the evidence and interpretations for the different approaches.
   ◆ Conclude by assessing the relative merits of the two approaches and make a judgement which links back to the original question.

3 Fascists and Italian society

The nature and ideology of Fascism and its impact on Italy

Key points

◆ Was Fascism merely Mussolini-ism?
◆ What were the implications of the nature of Fascism for Italian society under Mussolini?
◆ In what ways and with what success did Mussolini attempt to transform Italian society?

Was Fascism merely Mussolini-ism?

There is ongoing debate amongst historians about what constituted the nature of Italian Fascist beliefs. This is due to the fact that the Fascist Party (PNF), as unified by Mussolini, appeared to lack a defining philosophy. Mussolini recognised the problem when he commented that 'Fascism is too subtle a body of ideas to be understood by laymen or foreigners'. Some might add that Fascism was also too subtle to be understood by Mussolini, most Fascists and the average Italian in the inter-war years. This has led some historians to suggest that, for Mussolini, there was no real ideology underlying Fascism. It was merely 'a technique for winning power' (D. Mack Smith, quoted in *Modern History Review*, 1990) and 'a patchwork of bits and pieces collected from friend and foe' (D. Mack Smith, *Modern Italy*, 1997).

These views tend to suggest that Mussolini cynically manipulated a ragbag of ideas, drawing from it whatever enhanced his power and then discarding anything that appeared unpopular and ineffective. Such twists and turns suggest the total absence of any underlying philosophy in Mussolini's mind. The mixed coalition that was the PNF offered him a muddled collection of different beliefs and blueprints for society. Fascism as an idea did not exist.

The history of Mussolini's leadership certainly suggests there is some basis for this viewpoint:

◆ In 1919 he espoused a form of socialism, advocating abolition of private property, redistribution of land to the peasants, worker control of factories, progressive taxes on capital and the seizure of Church land. To cap it all he rejected dictatorship and militarism.

◆ The Conference on Fascist Culture, held at Bologna in 1925, gave little clear direction to the movement despite its production of the *Manifesto of Fascist Intellectuals*.

◆ By the time Mussolini defined Fascism in 1932, it had become authoritarian and militaristic, supporting reactionary capitalism. It had entered into an alliance with the Catholic Church and reduced the freedom of the working class.

◆ By the late 1930s, Mussolini added a Nazi-style racism to Fascism.

◆ Lastly, in 1943, he issued the Verona Manifesto which seemed to return to 1919, with a programme clearly borrowed from socialism.

It is understandable that some historians have concluded that Fascism, as defined by Mussolini, represented nothing more than 'Mussolini-ism', and was as changeable, opportunistic and inconsistent as the Duce himself. Its statements of belief were mere propaganda, made for effect and without any significant substance, a kind of ideology of shifting sound-bites. Furthermore, Mussolini's attempts to win support from the Italian elites by reducing the radical demands of the PNF appear to substantiate the accusation that by the late 1920s, the Fascist regime was becoming a reactionary state designed to protect the interests of capitalists and the other elites by reducing the influence of lower-class Italians. In short, the youthful radical Fascism of 1922 matured into a conservative middle age by 1932.

This version of events may be going too far. The radical characteristics of Fascism should not be so lightly dismissed. In the early 1930s, some within the PNF called for radical changes in Italian society and genuinely believed the PNF could become a revolutionary movement. For such Fascists, the hoped-for movement would regenerate the nation through the creation of a new Fascist youth, which would give rise to a transformed 'Fascist man' (*uomo fascista*). This 'Fascist man' – transformed through war and heroic deeds – would modernise Italian society and create a community united in its rejection of individualism, embracing instead the idea of a community totally obedient to the state. The work of the historian Lazzari in the 1980s highlighted the importance of images of rebirth in Fascist ideology. However, Fascists were remarkably vague about what the future Fascist society would look like. As one Fascist publication put it in 1927, Fascism represented 'the era of a new civilisation whose essence no one could know'.

In short, 'however pathetic, then squalid the Fascist regime turned out to be, its failures were not due to a lack of ideology. If anything, the original movement had accommodated too many rival versions of what it stood for ideologically' (R. Griffin, *The Nature of Fascism*, 1991). And many of these strands envisaged great changes in Italian society. Fascism therefore was much more than merely 'Mussolini-ism', or disguised conservatism. Whilst the Duce may have had no fixed beliefs and a tendency to please the elites, the PNF contained many ideologies, some of which were quite revolutionary. The best explanation for the shifting nature of Fascist ideology is that different groups within the movement had different degrees of influence over Mussolini at different times. The problem was that a regime whose supporters included radical *squadristi*, ex-socialists, nationalists and conservatives might rally wide-ranging support to start with, but could never present a unified plan of action and would ultimately dissatisfy some of its members, whatever it did.

What were the implications of the nature of Fascism for Italian society?

Fascism had many members who sincerely wanted to change, modernise and energise Italy. As we have seen, there was no consensus on how to do this. The movement itself also contained elements who did not envisage a shake-up of society. This meant that whilst Fascist social policy contained many attempts to change Italy, these attempts were rarely followed consistently and were often vague and lacking in clear policy. The fact that Mussolini's character reflected this lack of clear direction accelerated this chaotic process, but was not the only reason why chaos occurred.

The complex nature of the PNF led to conflicting policies on a wide range of ideas. A revealing example is the question of architecture. The more conservative architects, such as Marcello Piacenti and Ugo Ojetti, dreamed of vast monuments appropriate to a new Roman Empire. On the other hand, those architects in the group called the *Novecento* were influenced by the modern movement in architecture and wished to sweep away traditional concepts, replacing them with a rational and practical style. The most famous advocate of this approach was Giuseppe Pagano.

In what ways and with what success did Mussolini attempt to transform Italian society?

In 1938, Mussolini's son-in-law Galeazzo Ciano remarked 'the revolution must impinge upon the habits of Italians'. In order to assess how far Mussolini succeeded in doing this, it is necessary to look at different aspects of Italian life.

Religious belief

The Fascists never really knew how to cope with the Catholic Church. They had reached an understanding in the 1920s, but this did not resolve the profound differences between them. As time went on, these differences deepened into increasing mistrust. What is interesting is that, firstly, the achievement of Mussolini in reaching an agreement with the Vatican was built on positive work carried out by the Italian leader Vittorio Orlando between 1917 and 1919 and, secondly, the Fascists failed to really penetrate the Church.

For a while there seemed to be mutual benefits. During the Spanish Civil War, Pope Pius XI commented on how 'The first, the greatest and now the general peril, is certainly communism in all its forms and degrees'. This fear of communism was a common factor, but the Church disapproved of Mussolini's racial laws and actively used its own social groups to compete with the PNF for the loyalty of Italians. These social groups provided an alternative cultural focus, and the influence of groups such as Catholic Action increased after 1939. Consequently the Fascist alliance with the Church may have increased support for the regime, but in the long term it encouraged conservative trends and allowed the continuation of a counter-culture which rivalled the PNF.

Women and the family

Fascist attitudes to women tended to be very conservative. Mussolini commented that 'In our state, women must not count'. The Fascist preoccupation with creating a military culture meant that women were reserved the role of producing children in large quantities. In 1927, the so-called Battle for Births began. Its aim was to increase the Italian population from 40 to 60 million by 1950. Slogans such as women being 'angels of the hearth' were linked to practical discrimination such as:

◆ exempting families who had more than six children from taxation.

◆ giving marriage loans that were partly cancelled on each successive birth.

◆ ensuring that by the late 1930s civil service jobs and promotions were only open to married men.

◆ reducing women to no more than 10% of the total workforce by state discrimination after 1938.

These conservative attempts ended in failure. The birth rate actually declined until 1936, then rose a little, but by 1950 the Italian population stood at only 47.5 million. More than this, the Fascists were unable to prevent the spread of new ideas amongst women.

Education

Young people were targeted in the hope that they would form a new generation of Fascist youth. School textbooks were heavily censored. This increased after 1936, with 317 different history books reduced to a single government-approved text. Within schools, the stress was placed on Italian history and literature in order to imbue students with the Fascist version of culture and the past. The Ministry of Popular Culture banned all books considered 'unsuitable to the Fascist spirit'.

Outside school, a wide range of groups were set up to try to mould the minds of young people. The umbrella organisation of the ONB included the *Balilla* for boys aged 8–14, and the *Piccole Italiane* which covered girls of the same age. For those aged between 14 and 18, there was the *Avanguardisti* for boys and the *Giovani Italiane* for girls. In 1937 the ONB merged with the Young Fascists to form a unified party youth organisation, the GIL, which catered for all those aged between 6 and 21 years of age. From 1938 the GIL provided pre-military training as well as propaganda.

Despite these efforts to indoctrinate children, it has been estimated that 40% of all those aged between 8 and 18 managed to avoid joining these groups.

The Dopolavoro

Education – or re-education – was not confined to the young. Mussolini and the Fascist leadership wished to change the thinking of the entire Italian nation. In 1925, the Dopolavoro was set up with the clear aim of educating adults in Fascist modes of thinking. It aimed to provide leisure activities with a Fascist flavour, at the same time reducing worker irritation with the Fascist ban on trade union-sponsored clubs. By the 1930s, the activities of the Dopolavoro covered soccer, theatres, bands and libraries. Membership swelled from

300,000 in 1926 to nearly four million in 1939. Clubhouses were built in almost every town and village, and its activities became very popular indeed. This was helped by the fact that the organisation did not take its propaganda role too seriously, and so Italians could join without being treated to a diet of Fascist ideology. Many of the plays and other cultural activities put on by the Dopolavoro lacked much political content and were all the more popular for it.

The control of ideas

Mussolini put great effort into attempts to control ideas. It has even been suggested than Fascism was 'propaganda as a substitute for action' (D. Mack Smith, quoted in *Modern History Review*, 1990). In other words, Fascist claims far outstripped their real achievements. In time the most complex issues were reduced to catch phrases: 'He who has steel has bread', 'Nothing is won in history without bloodshed', 'Better to live one day as a lion than a hundred years as a sheep'. In order to convey these ideas the media was strictly controlled. Exceptional Decrees in 1926 and 1928 banned many newspapers. Journalists were forced to register with the Fascist Journalist Association. Mussolini spent much of his working day supervising the press and manufacturing a false view of reality. Indeed, all the leading Fascists had journalistic experience. In these efforts Mussolini achieved a high degree of success:

◆ Shifts in Fascist ideology took place with no negative press response.

◆ Mussolini's imperial victories in Africa received wide coverage with no mention of the extermination of African civilians.

◆ Mussolini was presented as a totalitarian ruler who was truly in command of the nation.

Many of these propaganda successes were due to the active work of Minculpop, the Ministry of Popular Culture. Its aim was to oversee the way in which the regime was presented.

Yet this success papered over a regime which achieved little, and in the long term, propaganda was no substitute for real policies. It could in fact be very dangerous, as demonstrated when the military boasts of Mussolini concealed how unprepared for war Italy really was. Furthermore, it is clear that for all his control of the media, Mussolini failed to create a new Fascist outlook. He once suggested that his aim was to make Italians 'much less nice and more hateful'. Mussolini's failure to inspire popular enthusiasm for the Second World War may suggest he failed in this aim to a significant degree.

Surprisingly, some areas of the media slipped through the Fascist net. One such area was cinema, despite the setting up of a Film Institute in 1925 and an Office of Cinematography in 1934. This was because much of the Italian film industry was privately owned, and Mussolini was reluctant to interfere with private capitalism despite his once radical rhetoric. Directors such as Pasqualino de Santis and Luchino Visconti continued working with considerable freedom.

A similar picture emerges with regard to higher intellectual work. 'In view of the fact that the Fascist regime interfered comparatively little with academic and intellectual freedom, nearly all the intellectuals were prepared to subscribe to Fascism and then continued as before with their intellectual and creative work' (J. Ridley, *Mussolini*, 1997). In many ways this sums up the Fascist impact on intellectual life – apparently overwhelming but in reality superficial.

Fascist racial policy

In 1931 there were only 50,000 Italian Jews, making up only 0.1% of the population. Anti-Semitism was not originally a Fascist theme, though a small minority of the leaders, such as Farinacci, were anti-Semites. Mussolini's longest-lasting mistress was Jewish. However, from 1938 Mussolini began to imitate his new Nazi friends. A Manifesto on Race made the bizarre claim that Italians were Nordic and Aryan. Intermarriage was banned, Jewish teachers and journalists lost their jobs, Jews faced property restrictions, were banned from state schools and universities, and Jews who had entered Italy since 1919 were repatriated.

These measures were very unpopular in Italy. The Pope condemned them, the laws were often ignored and police reports showed that Italians disapproved of them and resented German influence.

There is disagreement as to the relationship between Fascism and racism. It has often been said that it was little more than an attempt to copy the Germans – a kind of pledge of loyalty to the Axis – but which was not native to Italian Fascism. In support of this view, the lack of an Italian extermination programme to match the German Holocaust has often been cited.

However, the matter is more complex. While in one sense anti-Semitism was not a central element in Fascism, racism *was* implicit in it. The belief in Italian superiority was at the root of Fascism. The Fascists invited Italians to see themselves as having inherited the virtues of the Roman race. It gave rise to such outward manifestations as the Roman salute and the Roman step (a version of the Nazi goose step) and the concentration by some Fascist architects on classical building styles. This was much more than just emulating the ancient Roman Empire through a policy of expansionist empire-building and the encouragement of Roman themes. It was deeply arrogant, insisting that there was something uniquely superior about Italians which fitted them to subdue and rule other people. While this racism was less aggressive than the beliefs of the Nazis, it was still racism and capable of being manipulated to justify discrimination and atrocities.

In Africa, racist legislation predated the 1938 Manifesto on Race. Here it was based on white supremacy, and in 1935 in Eritrea and 1937 in Abyssinia, mixed black-white sexual relations were banned. Those who broke these laws faced prison sentences of five years. Furthermore, the mass slaughter of Africans in North Africa and in Abyssinia during Italian imperial expansion in the 1930s was a direct outworking of this racist view. This suggests that, as Jasper Ridley has commented, 'Mussolini became anti-Semitic without any pressure from the Germans because it was in the nature of Fascism to be anti-Semitic' (*Mussolini*, 1997). Or one might say it was in the nature of Fascism to be racist, and in the Europe of the late 1930s racism was frequently, but not exclusively, expressed as anti-Semitism.

Creating a classless Italian society?

Many of these attempts to mould Italian society aimed to dissolve the divisions caused by class. The more radical Fascists hoped that the new Fascist man would transcend class divisions and make them meaningless. Amongst ex-*squadristi* leaders such as Farinacci, there was a real belief that the old Italy would give way to a new one, in which all that mattered was a person's relationship with the state. They emphasised that it was a common experience of war and Fascist revolution that united the *squadristi*, and this was more fundamental than any other social characteristics.

However, these radicals were not the only influences on the direction taken by the PNF. Within the party there were other far more conservative forces. To these conservatives, the main preoccupation was the defence of traditional values and the crushing of communist revolution.

After 1922, the influence of the radicals declined and the conservative Fascists became more influential. The decline of the radicals was linked to the decline of the influence of the PNF itself and the increasing growth in Mussolini's personal dictatorship and cult of personality. Despite this, the tension between radicals and conservatives was never fully resolved, and Mussolini himself wavered between the two extremes.

How successful was the Fascist attempt to transform Italian society?

Fascism, as we have seen, was both a radical and a conservative force. With regard to women and the family it was socially conservative, and its alliance with the Catholic Church encouraged conservative trends. With regard to youth and propaganda, as well as racism, it attempted to be a revolutionary force, out to change Italian outlooks and beliefs. Of the two forces, it was in theory predominantly – but not consistently – revolutionary in its social aims. Whether this was true of its economic objectives remains to be seen in Chapter 4.

But how successful was Fascism as a revolutionary force? The answer must be that it achieved far less than might have been expected. Many children left school – and the control of the state – at 11 years. There was no Fascist penetration of private and Catholic schools. Despite the efforts of the Dopolavoro the regime made little headway in its efforts to win the hearts and minds of Italian workers. The upsurge of communist resistance in northern Italy after 1943 reveals the survival of socialist ideas and 'traditions which had outlasted twenty years of Fascist dictatorship and which now identified themselves with the Soviet Union' (T. Abse in R. Bessel (ed), *Fascist Italy and Nazi Germany: Comparison and Contrasts*, 1996).

By contrast there were some positive achievements:

◆ Medical care became more widely available, and more people were covered by schemes which offered pensions and unemployment benefit. There was also reduced infant mortality.

◆ There was greater access to sports and cultural facilities.

◆ A great school-building programme took place.

These factors help to explain the great loyalty felt towards the regime until the Second World War. But, as the next chapter will show, the economic position of the working class declined and earning power was down, resulting in much poverty. In short, Fascism had a significant impact on Italian society but fell far short of creating a new Italy. Most fundamentally:

◆ Fascism failed to destroy class divisions. Workers were exploited, and peasants were not integrated into wider society.

◆ Social barriers based on education became harder than ever to overcome. Elites kept power, and there was no common culture. It is significant that national Italian illiteracy rates did not fall below 20%, and in parts of southern Italy remained as high as 48%.

Figure 1
A heroic blackshirt is seen triumphant over a red flag (1936).

Figure 2
Another example of the manipulation of images. This example from the 1930s expresses the Fascist attitude towards both history and warfare.

Whether Mussolini would have been more successful had Fascism avoided war in Europe and consolidated its successes at home remains a more difficult question to answer. It is likely that, given its inherent contradictions and the resistance of Italian traditional culture, Fascism would never have worked the transformation it boasted. What is undisputed is that the Fascist longing for war resulted in the total destruction of what little success it did have.

Studying the impact of Fascism on Italian society

1 Study the two sources at Figures 1 and 2 above. For each, explain how ideas and images were manipulated in order to convey Fascist ideology.

2 Make notes on the following. In each case, discuss whether the aim was conservative or radical, and assess the extent of success:
   ◆ Fascist policy on youth
   ◆ Fascist policy on the Catholic Church
   ◆ Fascist policy on adult education
   ◆ Fascist policy on the mass media
   ◆ Fascist policy on race.

4 Mussolini and the Italian economy

Slogans in search of a philosophy?

Key points

- ◆ Did Mussolini have a clear plan for the running of the Italian economy?
- ◆ What patterns can be identified in Fascist economic policy, 1922–39?
- ◆ How successful was the Fascist regime in its management of the Italian economy?
- ◆ To what extent did the reality of Fascist economic policy fulfill its aims?

Did Mussolini have a clear plan for the running of the Italian economy?

Mussolini has become famous for his plans to control the Italian economy through government decisions. However, Denis Mack Smith speaks for a large number of historians when he claims that 'Fascism began with no particular economic policy: its doctrines of planned economy were one day to be called typically Fascist, but in fact they came as an afterthought' (*Modern Italy*, 1997). According to this interpretation, Mussolini in 1922 had only the objectives of:

- ◆ creating economic stability in order to ensure political stability.

- ◆ gaining support from the Italian elites by crushing communism, controlling working-class unrest, ensuring the protection of private profit and private property, and reducing government interference in the running of industry. *

- ◆ encouraging the expansion of those sectors of the Italian economy necessary for a military build-up and territorial expansion.

However, this may be too extreme a conclusion. Mussolini had been a member of the Socialist Party until 1914 and so was familiar with the concept of a planned economy, which meant a large role for government in economic organisation. The fact that Fascism was to develop such ideas of a planned economy into a distinct philosophy indicates that these ideas were part of the character of the movement from the start.

The matter though is complicated by both the character of Mussolini and of the Fascist Party (the PNF). Firstly, as has been clearly identified in Chapter 3, the PNF was a loose coalition of groups. This means that whilst it may be possible to detect clear strands in Fascist thinking, it would be a mistake to assume that all Fascists believed in these aims with the same intensity. Some even held contradictory beliefs. Furthermore, the character of Mussolini was such that, whilst there were clearly policies which were dearer to his heart than others, he had a tendency to chop and change depending on what best ensured his continued political survival. This was as true in economic policy as it was in social domestic policy and foreign policy.

The Corporate State

Despite the complex nature of Fascism, there was within its ranks a large number of members who believed that Fascism had a unique contribution to make to the development of the Italian economy. Their radical philosophy claimed that Fascism offered 'a Third Way between the anarchy of the liberal market economy and ... the Bolshevist planned one' (R. Griffin, *The Nature of Fascism*, 1991). This philosophy envisaged:

◆ the active involvement of the government in the planning and running of the economy in order to prevent the exploitation of the workers.

◆ harmony amongst all those involved in economic production.

◆ economic growth and expansion.

Such a radical solution would, it was hoped, stop working-class support for communism while keeping the support of the capitalists. It would also unite, involve and motivate Italian society, and ensure that the direction of economic policy was firmly in the hands of a radical Fascist administration. Such a new structure of both the economy and society was described as a 'Corporate State'.

Fascists claimed that this was a unique contribution to ideas about how an economy should be run. They were well aware that in the 1920s and 1930s there was considerable debate about whether governments should control their economies (as in the Five Year Plans of the USSR in the 1930s), or let them develop on their own (as in the most extreme demands of capitalists). By adopting a policy which promised government involvement without it developing into communism, Fascists hoped to appeal to a wide range of people and steal support from communism and from traditional capitalism.

The significance of this economic objective within Fascist ideology is clear from the fact that attempts were made to begin implementing economic policy as early as 1926. In that year, government minister Alfredo Rocco's Labour Relations Law recognised seven branches of economic activity: industry, agriculture, internal transport, merchant shipping, banking, commerce and intellectual work. They were formed into syndicates, or corporations, controlled by the Ministry of Corporations. Only these groups would be recognised in bargaining with the representatives of Italian businessmen, the Confindustria (Confederation of Industry).

This action was intended to compensate workers for the loss of their independent trade unions, and the Fascist syndicates now became their representatives instead. The intention was that instead of dividing industry between workers and their bosses, all those involved within an area of the economy would be united in planning and organising the running of that area of national life. Disputes would be settled and objectives reached under the guidance of the Fascist state. In this way, class divisions would be replaced by industrial harmony and the peaceful settlement of disputes.

In 1930 a National Council of Corporations was set up. By 1934, this had further refined the system by recognising a total of twenty-two different groups within the economy. In 1939 this new economic system was united with the political system when a Chamber of Fasces and Corporations was set up to replace the existing parliamentary structure. This so-called Corporate State became one of the most characteristic features of Italian Fascism, and aroused great interest abroad.

What was Mussolini's role within these developments?

As we have seen, Mussolini's socialist background made him favour the idea of state intervention in a planned economy. It also left him with a radical tendency which desired revolutionary changes in Italian society. However, he never fully developed these tendencies, nor was he totally committed to them.

The real creators of the Corporate State were other Fascist thinkers. The most noteworthy was Edmondo Rossoni, who between 1919 and 1925 pushed hard for its implementation. As with a number of Fascist leaders, they were heavily influenced by the ideas of 'syndicalism' which had been prevalent in some areas of European trade unionism and socialism before the First World War. At its simplest, syndicalism called for:

◆ placing control of individual industries in the hands of unions of workers. These unions would include all the workers, and would control all aspects of the industries – production, sales and labour conditions.

◆ representatives of these unions to form the government of the country. Government would then be based on representatives from different industries, not on geographical constituencies.

Typically though, Rossoni's Fascist Left was only one strand in the complex tapestry of the PNF. Other Fascist leaders had their own view of the role of the Corporate State:

◆ Some leaders, such as Farinacci, favoured an Italy dominated by the PNF structure itself. To these Fascists, the corporations were of minor interest.

◆ More moderate leaders, such as Giuseppe Bottai, hoped that the corporations would eliminate class conflict, increase production and modernise Italy by making its industrial management more harmonious and efficient. To Fascists such as these, the corporations were economic instruments, not revolutionary instruments to use in the creation of a new government structure.

◆ To the more conservative nationalists such as Rocco, the Corporate State was a means by which socialist trade unionism could be destroyed and workers brought under the disciplined control of their employers. To these Fascists, the corporate structures were repressive tools in the hands of a conservative dictatorship.

Mussolini, sympathetic but uncommitted, held the ground between these various factions. At first he was content to let the left-wing radicals such as Rossoni have their way, but his desire to keep the support of the Italian elites and to keep power firmly in his own hands meant that he never allowed the Corporate State to develop fully. His final position was far closer to that of conservatives such as Rocco. Consequently, what might have been a revolutionary structure eventually settled down into being little more than another control mechanism to discipline the Italian workers and placate Italian capitalists.

What patterns can be identified in Fascist economic policy, 1922–39?

Phase 1, 1922–25: Caution and prosperity

Until 1925 the Fascist Left forced the pace within the movement, but only achieved limited success. This was at first due to the continued existence of independent trade unions and the unwillingness of the Confindustria to accept the radical demands of those who favoured the Corporate State. There was an apparent shift leftwards in 1923 with the Chigi Palace Pact, which promised the Fascist Labour Confederation exclusive bargaining rights with employers. But the employers failed to keep their side of the bargain, and Mussolini's government – not wishing to do anything too radical – refused to intervene decisively in favour of the corporations.

This was a boom period when Italian exports increased and the government reduced spending, cut taxes on companies and reduced state involvement in the economy. Mussolini was determined not to alienate wealthy Italian businessmen, and the improvement in working-class living standards in this period were due to the favourable economic conditions, not government intervention.

Phase 2, 1925–30: Radical false-start, compromise and risk

In 1925 a new agreement with Confindustria – the Vidoni Palace Pact – recognised only Confindustria and the Fascist Labour Confederation as the representatives respectively of capitalists and workers. Rival trade unions were banned. However this apparent Fascist radicalism did not last. Rocco's Labour Relations Law (April 1926) and the Labour Charter (1927) ensured that it was the state which dominated the corporations. Furthermore, the system clearly favoured the employers. The Ministry of Corporations was not allowed to expand its role into economic planning, which was jealously guarded by the Economics Ministry.

This left the Ministry of Corporations only the role of administering the syndicates and settling labour disputes. Even in this area it found it lacked the power to dictate to industrialists, and Italian workers were powerless to change this. In 1928 the Fascist Labour Confederation was broken up into six parts which put an end to any power and influence it still had. The brief radical phase had ended.

A more confident Mussolini began to intervene in the economy without actually reducing the power of industrialists. At times between 1922 and 1925, the exchange rate had dropped as low as 150 lire to the pound. In 1927 Mussolini insisted on a new value of 90 lire to the pound, a policy known as 'Quota 90'. This looked impressive, as it made the Italian currency seem powerful. However, it severely damaged Italian export industries since it made Italian goods more expensive abroad. For workers, this drop in exports led to longer working hours and cuts in wages.

The Italian textile industry was particularly badly hit. Car manufacturing suffered too, as it relied on selling many of its products abroad. The great Fiat company was exporting fewer cars in the 1930s than in the 1920s – a direct result of Quota 90. There were, however, benefits for middle-class Italians on fixed incomes, whose purchasing power increased. Additionally, Mussolini put tariffs on imports to protect Italian industries. This benefited steel, armaments and shipbuilding, but made food expensive and damaged the standard of living of ordinary people.

A more successful policy appeared to be the so-called 'Battle for Grain', which was launched in 1925 to increase grain production. This would serve two main purposes:

◆ It would stop Italy relying on foreign grain supplies. This was very important if war broke out, since Italy would starve if foreign grain were cut off.

◆ It would improve the prosperity of Italian farmers. To achieve an increase in grain production, government grants were given to farmers to buy tractors and fertiliser, along with free advice on the latest farming methods.

These incentives had the desired effect. In the early 1920s, Italian grain production had stood at 5.5 million tonnes a year. By the early 1930s this had risen to over 7 million tonnes. Mussolini was filmed working alongside harvesters and enjoyed the credit for the great achievement. There was, however, a down-side to the story, as much of the land would have been better suited to the production of citrus fruits, grapes and olive oil. Furthermore, the success had only been made possible by increased taxes to cover subsidies to farmers.

A similar propaganda triumph was the draining of the Pontine Marshes. The aim was to remove an area of malaria-infested marshes and, at the same time, provide sites for farms run by ex-servicemen. This was a success, improving public health and providing jobs for many thousands during the Depression. It also provided many propaganda opportunities for Mussolini to be photographed at work amongst his people. However, it needs to be remembered that the amount of land drained was relatively small, and so the extent of this success should not be exaggerated.

Phase 3, 1930–35: State intervention and loss of worker power

In response to the Depression of the 1930s, Mussolini's government intervened in the economy on a large scale. The state funded the construction of motorways and hydro-electric plants, and compensated banks for losses of money loaned to industry. An Institute for Industrial Reconstruction (IRI) was established to provide loans to industry and to take responsibility for loss-making industries such as iron, steel and shipbuilding. These actions reduced some of the worst impacts of the Depression but were very costly to the tax payer.

Despite these actions, two million people remained unemployed, and although the Corporate State continued to develop, it was little more than an empty shell. From 1928, the workers no longer decided on their own representatives in the corporations, and the job of representing the workers was taken over by party officials. As a result, decisions were often made which favoured businessmen at the expense of the workers. The Corporate State had become a structure for oppression and exploitation. As Gaetano Salvemini commented in 1936, to try to assess what the corporations did was like 'looking in a dark room for a black cat which is not there'.

In the countryside, despite Fascist claims of being the champions of small peasants, only 0.5% of the population owned about 42% of the land. Once more, Mussolini's regime preserved the privileged position of the very rich.

Phase 4, 1935–39: Expanding capitalists, autarky and crisis

From 1935, the League of Nations' sanctions against Italy following the invasion of Abyssinia encouraged a trend towards self-sufficiency, or 'autarky'. This was a trend whose roots lay in the late 1920s. It benefited industries that were required for military expansion such as steel, chemicals and shipbuilding, because the government purchased their products. Basic foodstuff industries also benefited, with Italians having to purchase food at home rather than having the freedom to buy from abroad. At the same time, capitalists were allowed considerable freedom to expand. Fiat was allowed a virtual monopoly in car production, as was Pirelli in rubber. It is clear that Mussolini's combined desire for military expansion and the support of wealthy and powerful Italians had submerged all previous radical experiments.

By 1940 this policy had reached a crisis point. Self-sufficiency had not been achieved and the government faced huge budget deficits. The answer was either to cut military expenditure or living standards. Mussolini was unable to resolve the crisis, and entered a war of conquest as a way out of the dilemma. This was to be an escape route leading to catastrophe.

How successful was the Fascist regime in its management of the economy?

Mussolini's government did have some positive economic achievements:

◆ The new *autostrada*, or motorways, proved to be very efficient.

◆ Electrified railways led to the boast that Italian trains ran on time.

◆ Industrial output increased. Between 1936 and 1940, industry overtook agriculture as the single largest contributor to GNP, increasing from 29% to 34%. State-owned monopolies stimulated new mineral resources, developed natural fibres, improved efficiency in the petro-chemical industry and reduced coal and oil imports through hydroelectric schemes.

However, to be set against these achievements there were major failings:

◆ Mussolini ignored the structural problems of Italy. There was great rural poverty and the north-south divide continued. Italy remained industrially underdeveloped with low productivity, high costs, a decline in domestic consumption and a slow recovery from the Depression.

◆ Confindustria dominated industry, exploiting workers and small firms.

◆ There were too few consumer goods.

◆ Preparation for war slowed economic recovery and failed to prepare Italy adequately. Though industrial output was up, Italy lagged behind Britain, France and Germany, and could not cope with the losses of war.

To what extent did the reality of Fascist economic policy fulfil its aims?

Mussolini never established a definite set of economic aims. Nevertheless, it is clear that between 1922 and 1926 he allowed the more radical Fascists to construct the basis of the Corporate State and, furthermore, he permitted this idea of the Fascist state to continue developing and evolving. Thus it seems fair to say that while Fascism did not possess a clear set of economic goals in 1922, Mussolini had allowed a set to appear by 1926. To this extent there was, from the mid 1920s, a distinctive Fascist proposal for the direction that Italian economic, political and social development should take.

To what extent did Fascism fulfil these aims? The clear answer is that it failed to do so monumentally. The Corporate State became nothing more than a propaganda exercise which masked the exploitation of the workers. Whilst Mussolini never gave up his belief in state intervention as a modernising force, the intervention which took place had only very limited impact on the direction of Italian economic development. It failed to address Italy's structural problems, lacked clarity, did not integrate workers into the economic (or political) system and, whilst setting boundaries to industrial growth, allowed capitalist enterprises a relatively free hand within those boundaries to pursue their own profit. Mussolini's obsession with an economic policy that would sustain foreign policy adventures finally dominated all other objectives, and ultimately failed to achieve its goals.

This is not to say there were no achievements. Rather, it is to assess them as achievements on a small scale, compared to the betrayal of the apparent radical objectives of the Corporate State and the ultimate failure of the Italian economy to sustain the unrealistic demands that Mussolini's foreign policy placed on it.

Studying Mussolini and the Italian economy

1 Make notes on each of the following, explaining its significance for the economic policy of Mussolini's government:
- ◆ Quota 90
- ◆ The Battle for Grain
- ◆ Autarky.

2 From what you have read:
- ◆ explain the aims of the 'Corporate State'.
- ◆ produce a time-line of the main events in its development. Identify what you consider to be the turning points in its development and why.
- ◆ suggest to what extent you agree with the view that the Corporate State 'was a travesty of what it purported to be' (A. Cassels, *Fascist Italy*, 1969).

3 What arguments can be offered for and against the view of Mack Smith on Mussolini's grasp of economics that 'he had little understanding of the subject and not much interest in it' (D. Mack Smith, *Mussolini*, 1981)?

 # Italian foreign policy 1922–45

A dream of Empire but no plan?

Key points

◆ Problems in analysing the aims and direction of Italian foreign policy
◆ What are the key events in Italian foreign policy?
◆ What alternative options have been suggested by historians to explain the character of Italian foreign policy?
◆ Why did Italy go to war in 1940?
◆ Why did Italy lose the Second World War?

What problems face historians in attempting to identify the aims and direction of Italian foreign policy?

Historians face a number of serious problems in their efforts to identify the main aims of Italian foreign policy in the 1920s and 1930s. At first glance this is unexpected, since Mussolini made foreign policy a major part of his political strategies, devoting a great deal of time to it and allowing it to dominate the character and direction of the Fascist state in the 1930s. A great many of his speeches and public pronouncements at this time were preoccupied with issues of foreign policy. This would suggest that the available data should be varied and widespread, allowing a fairly confident analysis of what he and the Fascist movement aimed to do in this area.

In fact, this is not the case at all. As with so many of his public utterances, Mussolini was long on rhetoric, and short on detail and definitive statements. Claims made in 1922 that 'foreign policy is the area which especially preoccupies us … [to] make Italy great, respected and feared' clearly suggest that an expansionist foreign policy lay at the heart of Mussolini's ambitions, but tell us nothing about:

◆ the specific goals of such expansionism.

◆ the methods to be employed.

◆ the orientation of Italy towards other states.

◆ whether there was anything uniquely Fascist about these ambitions.

In short, as with so much in Fascist Italy, the historian is left with a lot of noise suggesting general ambitions but little in terms of specific policy that can be firmly analysed. This situation is compounded by the apparent twists and turns in Italian foreign policy which, coupled with the equally changeable and dramatic foreign policy statements by Mussolini, suggest a wide range of possible motives and aims. Some of these appear contradictory, some opportunistic, and some ideological. As a result, there are a number of different options which have been suggested by historians as attempts to make sense of this complex and confused situation. Not surprisingly, they are as varied and contradictory as the evidence that they attempt to make sense of.

The matter is further complicated by the fact that Mussolini consciously tried to suggest that Fascist Italy represented a sharp break with the immediate Liberal past, playing up anything that seemed different about Fascist actions and ignoring much of what had been achieved by his predecessors. There are direct parallels here with Hitler's foreign policy versus the foreign policy of Weimar and the earlier Germany of the Kaiser. However, with Mussolini there is a strong case for suggesting that his interest in expanding Italian influence in the Balkans, the Mediterranean and Africa simply continued themes that had influenced Italian foreign policy since the late 19th century.

This continuity can be partly explained by the fact that, in an attempt to avoid alienating the existing elites in Italian society, there was no Fascist purge of the Italian Foreign Ministry and diplomatic service. Whilst key jobs went to the newly arrived Fascist leadership (as one would expect), many of the essential jobs remained with the same men who had served Italian governments before 1922 and indeed during and before the First World War. There were of course significant tensions between ambitious Fascists and these representatives of the 'old Italy'. The very existence of such tensions suggests that these old elites continued to be very influential and were a force for continuity within Italian foreign policy.

Mussolini was clearly determined that Italy should finally gain the rewards that had escaped her at the end of the First World War. These rewards lay in expanding Italian influence around the Adriatic and the Balkans, and enlarging Italian colonial territories in East Africa. In this, Mussolini was encouraged by the Fascist dream of creating a new Roman Empire with the Duce in the position of Emperor. However, as with his other ambitions, the route to this objective was not clear.

Key events in Italian foreign policy

The quiet years, 1922–34

The early years of Fascism saw a general attempt by Mussolini to work within the existing international system rather than challenge it. This is not to say that Mussolini did not take opportunities to increase Italian power and influence. However, he did so cautiously and with an eye to the attitudes of the more powerful countries in Europe, namely Britain and France.

The period 1922–34 began with an exception to this cautious approach. In 1923, Mussolini attempted to use brute force to gain concessions from Greece over the murder of an Italian general and four of his staff while they were settling a boundary dispute between Greece and Albania. Mussolini demanded compensation in the form of 50 million lire from Greece. When the Greeks refused, he ordered the bombardment and consequent occupation of the island of Corfu.

The British led the other European powers in opposing this Italian aggression, and Mussolini was forced to give up Corfu. He did receive the 50 million lire compensation, but not a full apology from Greece. The episode showed that Italy was not strong enough to resist the more powerful countries of Europe. Mussolini would clearly need to work with Britain rather than against her in pursuing his ambitions – at least in the short term.

The Corfu incident persuaded Mussolini to be more cautious, but it did not prevent him from attempting to extend Italian power and influence. In 1924 he succeeded in bringing enough diplomatic pressure on Yugoslavia to make her sign the Pact of Rome. This gave the city of Fiume to Italy, which Italian nationalists had been demanding since the end of the First World War.

Mussolini was determined that Italy should dominate Yugoslavia, and resented the French influence prevalent there. In 1924, the Italians backed an Albanian chieftain called Zog so that he became king of Albania. By 1926 Albania was virtually under Italian control, though officially independent. Since Albania bordered Yugoslavia, this was a careful policy designed to intimidate that state. Italy then proceeded to supply money to the Croats, who wished to break away from Yugoslavia and form an independent Croatian state.

These efforts reveal that Mussolini was determined to bully and use force to dominate Italy's weaker neighbours, but he had realised this had to be done in a way which did not openly challenge the British and French. As part of this more careful approach to international diplomacy, Mussolini:

◆ remained in the League of Nations.

◆ guaranteed the Locarno Pact in 1925, which confirmed the permanence of Germany's western borders.

◆ signed the Kellogg Pact in 1928, which promised to reject war as a way of settling disputes.

◆ negotiated with Britain to settle the border between British-controlled Egypt and Italian-controlled Libya.

Mussolini's apparent moderation won him support from Britain and France, flattered him with an image as an international statesman and offered the possibility of concessions from the British and French. This seemed the best approach in the face of united opposition by Britain and France to Italian aggression. Besides which, there was no other country in Europe that Italy could work with against the British and French in the 1920s.

Behind the scenes though, Mussolini was secretly at work to make friends amongst other nationalities who, like Italy, wished to revise the peace treaties:

◆ He signed a friendship treaty with Hungary in 1927.

◆ He secretly trained German pilots and funded right-wing German groups in the hope of bringing a Fascist government to power in Germany.

Mussolini clearly hoped that a strong Germany would frighten the British and French. He imagined that this would make them sympathetic to Italian demands in order to prevent Italy becoming an ally of this new Germany. On the other hand, once Adolf Hitler had come to power in 1933, Mussolini did not want Germany to become too powerful. He particularly did not want Germany to dominate Austria.

To avoid an *Anschluss* (union) between Germany and Austria, Mussolini gave support to the Austrian leader, Englebert Dollfuss, who also feared an

Anschluss. In 1934 Dollfuss was assassinated by Austrian Nazis. Mussolini rushed Italian troops to the border with Austria to oppose any attempt by Hitler to use the crisis as an opportunity to take over Austria.

In 1935 Italy joined Britain and France in the Stresa Front. This committed the three nations to oppose any future German breaches of international treaties. Clearly, Mussolini was prepared to work with the Western democracies against Hitler for the time being. But he had a price for this cooperation. The price was that Britain and France would allow him to build an African Empire.

The Abyssinian crisis

Mussolini hoped that an Empire in Africa would lead to Italy becoming one of the great powers. He had a number of objectives:

◆ Military prestige would enhance his position as Duce.

◆ Italy would be respected and feared by other nations.

◆ Italians unable to prosper in Italy could become colonists in Africa.

◆ African people would swell the size of the Italian army.

◆ The Italian economy would benefit from new markets and resources.

The target for Italian aggression was Abyssinia (modern Ethiopia). It was one of only two African states which had not been conquered by Europeans. Furthermore, it lay next to the Italian colonies of Eritrea and Somaliland.

There was a history of tension between Italy and Abyssinia over the exact course of the border between Abyssinia and the neighbouring Italian colonies. As far back as 1896, Italian attempts to dominate Abyssinia had led to Italian humiliation at the battle of Adowa. Italy had continued to try to dominate Abyssinia in the 1920s, sponsoring her joining the League of Nations in 1923 and signing a friendship treaty with her in 1928, while all the time making plans to conquer her.

The opportunity for conquest came in 1934, when Italian and Abyssinian troops clashed at the oasis of Wal-Wal. Abyssinia appealed to the League for an enquiry, but Mussolini launched an invasion in October 1935. By April 1936 the Italians had captured the capital, Addis Ababa, and the Abyssinian Emperor Haile Selassie was forced to flee. The Italian conquest was achieved through brutal methods ranging from use of poison gas to the massacre of whole villages.

The conquest of Abyssinia made Mussolini very popular in Italy, but it was eventually to cause a crisis in his relationship with Britain and France. The League of Nations condemned the conquest, and Britain and France supported the use of sanctions against Italy. However, these sanctions were weak and ineffective because they did not include banning sales of steel, oil and coal to Italy. Furthermore, Britain did not close the Suez Canal to Italy, which would have cut Italy off from Abyssinia. Clearly the Western democracies did not want a confrontation. Nevertheless, Mussolini was angered by their opposition. In December 1935 the British and French suggested a compromise, the Hoare-Laval Pact, which would have given Italy the vast majority of Abyssinia. It failed because public opinion in the two countries was outraged at this apparent rewarding of Italian aggression.

By the end of the Abyssinian crisis Mussolini had become alienated from the British and French, whilst at the same time deciding that they lacked the real strength of character to stand up to him. No longer associated with the European democracies and convinced of their general weakness, Italy soon saw friendship with Germany as the best way to force concessions from Britain and France. The conquest of Abyssinia was to change the direction of European diplomacy in the 1930s. It was therefore a decisive step towards the Second World War.

Italy and the Spanish Civil War

The extent to which Mussolini had drifted away from his friendship with the Western democracies was clearly illustrated by his response to the Spanish Civil War (1936–39). Both German and Italian troops fought on the side of the right-wing Spanish Nationalists. Although cautious at first, Mussolini began to send Italian soldiers to Spain from early 1937. Eventually he sent some 50,000 troops to assist the defeat of the elected Republican government. For Mussolini, a Spanish Nationalist victory offered a number of possibilities:

◆ It would extend Italian influence to Spain.

◆ Mussolini could gain the credit for helping to defeat communism in Spain.

◆ He hoped to weaken British naval power in the western Mediterranean.

◆ France would be flanked by hostile states – Spain, Germany, Italy.

◆ Italy could test the efficiency of its armed forces in Spain.

Britain and France adopted a policy of non-intervention but were unable to stop other foreign troops from getting involved (as well as the Germans and Italians supporting the Nationalists, the USSR sent assistance to the Republican government). The significance of the Spanish Civil War was that it further demonstrated the weakness of the Western democracies and it saw Germany and Italy clearly placed on the same side. The balance of power in Europe was shifting further and, despite his continuing misgivings about Hitler, Mussolini was drifting more and more into the German camp in European affairs.

Fascist Italy and Nazi Germany

After 1936 Mussolini – who had first opposed the expansionism of the Nazis – moved into alliance with Hitler. It was a move which seemed to promise Italy the best advantage. In the so-called Rome–Berlin Axis (1936), Italy was promised a free hand to expand in the Mediterranean, whilst agreeing to support German ambitions in eastern Europe. It was a friendship taken further in the Anti-Comintern Pact of 1937, which appealed to both Hitler and Mussolini's hatred of communism and the USSR.

During the Czech crisis of 1938 Mussolini acted as a 'neutral' chairman for the Munich Conference, when Hitler was given the Sudetenland. This appealed to Mussolini's view of himself as an international statesman, but of course he was far from neutral, actively cooperating with Hitler in order to ensure that the Munich deal gave Hitler what he wanted.

However, it was clear that not only was Italy a junior partner in the friendship, but that Hitler had no intention of briefing Mussolini before his major actions. There was no consultation with Italy over either the *Anschluss* (1938) or the final German occupation of what remained of Czechoslovakia in March 1939. These high-handed German actions annoyed Mussolini but did not shift him from his judgement that Italian ambitions would only be met through cooperation with an aggressive Germany.

This judgement was reinforced in April 1939. Following the Italian invasion of Albania, Britain and France guaranteed the security of Greece and Turkey. These were areas which Mussolini considered to be in the Italian sphere of influence. It was evident that the Western democracies would not support Italian expansion at the expense of these countries. Consequently, although Mussolini made an agreement with Britain over preserving the status quo in the Mediterranean in 1938 and carried on with half-hearted negotiations with France in 1939, he was clearly not going to be shaken from his dependence on Germany. Indeed, Italian demands in 1939 on French territory, in the form of Nice, Corsica and Tunis, are best understood as the bullying demands of a dictator who thought he had joined the winning side in European diplomacy.

War, though, was not exactly what Mussolini had in mind. It carried too many risks for a state as unprepared as Italy. Yet such was Mussolini's lack of elementary caution that he willingly joined Germany in the Pact of Steel, in May 1939, even though it committed him to support Germany in a war which Germany might start whenever Hitler chose.

Pressure on Mussolini by his Foreign Office led to desperate attempts by Italy to backtrack from this dangerous commitment. Before May was out, an anxious note was sent to Hitler pointing out the fact that Italy was not prepared for war. The Germans did not even bother to reply. In August, as the German-manufactured crisis with Poland escalated, Mussolini once again tried desperately to avoid being dragged into a war, the outcome of which was anyone's guess. Hitler demanded that Italy stick by its promise. The Italians responded with a vast list of requirements which would have to be met before they entered into war in 1939.

Hitler invaded Poland on 1 September 1939. The Western democracies declared war on 3 September. Mussolini – who had tried without success to arrange another Munich-style conference to avoid war while satisfying German demands – backed out of his promises made in the Pact of Steel and remained neutral.

Alternative options to explain Italian foreign policy, 1922–39

Italian foreign policy was clearly complex. The same Italian state that cooperated with the Western democracies at Locarno and Stresa declared war on them in 1940. The same Italian state which had threatened to make 'the Brenner bristle with bayonets' to prevent German union with Austria eventually accepted the *Anschluss* and entered the war on the side of Germany, once an arch-rival and apparent enemy. Faced with the complexities of Italian foreign policy, historians have suggested a number of different ways to interpret and make sense of it in terms of its directions and aims. These different options offer some radically different alternatives.

Option 1: Mussolini – the unprincipled destabiliser

This is a view associated with, amongst others, Denis Mack Smith. In brief, the view holds that Mussolini had no permanent principles. His overriding aim was to gain advantage for himself and Italy by any combination of actions which suited him at the time. Any advantage Italy gained automatically reflected on him as the Duce, and so his vanity and ambition became fused with the foreign policy of the state. Since it did not matter to Mussolini which route was taken to enhancing his reputation as a powerful leader, he would seize whatever opportunity presented itself at any given time. In the 1920s he pretended to be pro-British and a respectable diplomat because he felt Italy was not strong enough to take advantage of international opportunities without the help, or approval, of the British. However, even at this time he was already embarking on a policy of creating or encouraging instability anywhere that suited him. It was a policy deliberately targeted 'to create tensions and destabilise other countries' (D. Mack Smith, 1990). This was because he had decided that only in a situation of unrest and conflict could a state as weak as Italy gain advantage by playing off the other powers against each other.

Evidence for this can be found in the following:

◆ Mussolini's training of German military pilots in direct violation of the Treaty of Versailles.

◆ His initial support for German right-wing groups in the hope that a resurgent Germany would break up European stability.

◆ His smuggling arms across Europe and indeed the world to fuel unrest in places as diverse as Austria, Hungary, the Balkans, Afghanistan, Yemen and China.

It was opportunism such as this that caused him first to side with the democracies at Stresa when he felt he might use their fear of Germany to force concessions from them, but later to support Germany when he assessed Britain and France as being incapable of withstanding Hitler. In the latter situation, he felt he might gain more from helping an increasingly aggressive Germany.

Option 2: Mussolini – the lost ally of the democracies

This assessment of Mussolini's actions is associated to a large extent with Richard Lamb, and to a smaller extent with the work of the Italian historian, Renzo de Felice. In its most clearly stated form, this view holds that, with the exception of the Corfu incident, Mussolini:

> 'aligned Italian foreign policy with Britain's until the Abyssinian war in 1935. He had ample reason to expect Britain to condone his invasion of Abyssinia; hence it was a great shock to him when under the Covenant of the League of Nations Britain took the lead over imposing economic sanctions on Italy. Once his conquest was complete he tried to renew his friendship with Britain; only when his overtures were spurned did he turn to Hitler, whom he disliked and feared' (R. Lamb, *Mussolini and the British*, 1997).

Within Option 2 there are variations. Lamb sees Mussolini as sincere in his desire to court Britain. According to Lamb, Mussolini had been encouraged in his ambitions towards Abyssinia by informal arrangements with both the British and French since the early 1920s. The failure of Britain and France to discuss the matter of Abyssinia with him at Stresa only encouraged his belief that he had a free hand in East Africa. His actions therefore were not designed to antagonise or challenge these nations, but were taken in the sincere belief that they would willingly allow him to pursue his dream of an East African Empire.

The opposition of Britain and France therefore came as a real shock, and Mussolini felt genuinely outraged by what he saw as their betrayal. When, after the Abyssinian invasion, he attempted to re-establish a front against Hitler (whose designs on Austria were feared by Italy as a threat on their northern frontier), he found the British unwilling to work with him. It was with reluctance that he shifted his position in order to work with Germany.

The position of de Felice is more of a combination of Option 1 and Option 2. For de Felice, Mussolini was genuinely willing to work with the British but was enough of an opportunist to keep his options fully open. Consequently, if Britain had acted differently after 1936, Mussolini might have been kept in the anti-German alliance embodied in the Stresa Front. According to de Felice, even as late as 1940 Mussolini was not fully committed to the German alliance, and toyed with the idea of switching to a position of supporting Britain and France.

Option 3: Mussolini – the traditional Italian

As has already been noted, there is some evidence to suggest that Mussolini followed several aspects of traditional Italian foreign policy. His main areas of interest were in the Balkans, along the Danube and in Africa. These were areas where previous Italian governments had also tried to exert control (with regard to Africa) or extend their influence (with regard to south-eastern and central Europe). In this there were great similarities between the priorities of Fascist Italy and those of earlier right-wing Liberals and nationalists. Philip Morgan has assessed Mussolini's aims as being 'not so much Fascist as Italian' and concluded that 'Fascist foreign policy could be seen as conventional or the extension of a certain trend' (*Italian Fascism*, 1995).

However, as well as inheriting the direction of traditional foreign policy, Mussolini also inherited its weaknesses. Mussolini, like previous Italian governments, had to face the reality that Italy lacked the economic muscle to impose its will on other countries. Hence two significant features of both Mussolini's and earlier Italian governments' foreign policy were that:

◆ Italy needed the active assistance or consent of other more powerful nations if she were to achieve her ambitions.

◆ Italy was most influential when she was able to exploit the tensions and rivalries between other states. This meant she could force concessions from allies as the price for Italian support, or make the most of other states being distracted by problems.

This whole approach has been summed up by Morgan as 'makeweight diplomacy'. This means Italy could add its weight to other countries in order to get things done, but was not strong enough to do this on its own.

Option 4: Mussolini – the prisoner of his domestic problems

Option 4 suggests that there was no real substance to Mussolini's foreign policy other than the desire to enthuse Italians in order to bind them closer to the Fascist regime. As such, it was driven by domestic needs. By the end of the 1920s Fascism had failed to transform Italian society. In Mussolini's opinion, the Italians had failed to display the enthusiasm for military discipline and the transformation of Italy that he had dreamed of. Consequently, he tried to use the experience of war as a way of 'creating the new Fascism after the conquest of the Empire' (Renzo de Felice, *Fascism: An Informal Introduction to its Theory and Practice*, 1976). This offered a way of both diverting the attention of the Italian public from the economic failures of Fascism and seizing raw materials and markets which could benefit the Italian economy. As such, imperial expansion offered a way to both 'galvanise the masses and try to break the vicious circle of economic crisis' (G. Carocci, *Italian Fascism*, 1974).

Making sense of the evidence

Perhaps the most convincing explanation of Mussolini's foreign policy lies in a combination of Options 1, 3 and 4. This would leave us with a unprincipled opportunist, whose freedom of action was restricted by the basic economic weaknesses of Italy and, strikingly, by his willingness to believe his own fantastic boasts whilst despairing of transforming Italy into a nation of Fascists. Mussolini's first phase of reasonable diplomacy (with the exception of Corfu) could then be explained by Italy's weaknesses and the stability of the post-war settlement in the 1920s. However, his underlying opportunism is revealed in the fact that even then he was involved in encouraging tensions, hoping to exploit the possibilities they raised. The rise of Nazi Germany and the problems of the Depression gave him opportunities to play 'makeweight diplomacy'. First he played it with Britain and France against Germany. Later he played it with Germany against the democracies. In the former situation he was genuinely fearful of Germany. In the latter situation he had judged the democracies to be lacking in the necessary commitment to stop Germany, and so shifted position to line up behind Germany in order to gain from the chaos this seemed likely to cause. The problem for Mussolini was that this lining up behind an increasingly aggressive and confident Nazi Germany cut away his room for manoeuvre. Increasingly he found himself dominated by Hitler, whilst unable to resist the prospect that easy prizes would fall to Italy if Germany were successful. His increasing entanglement in a relationship with Germany – always unpopular in Italy – was to lead him to destruction.

Why did Italy go to war in 1940?

The astonishing German victories of autumn 1939 and early summer 1940 dazzled Mussolini. They offered just the opportunities to steal easy victories that friendship with Germany had always promised. The problem was that since Italy had not entered the war in 1939, it could not seize any booty. Mussolini's Italy, of course, was as unprepared for war in 1940 as it had been in 1939. However, the prospect of seizing the fruits of victory without taking any risks now arose. Propelled by greed and a mistaken belief in Fascist Italy's strength, Mussolini joined the war in June 1940 by launching an invasion of France. It was the culmination of a policy of aggressive opportunism that had characterised Italian foreign policy in the 1930s.

Italy at war – from humiliation to disaster, 1940–43

Italy was not ready for war:

◆ Its equipment was inferior.

◆ It had few mechanised forces.

◆ Its army was poorly led.

◆ Most Italians disapproved of the alliance with Germany.

◆ Italy depended on Germany for its coal and iron ore. Kept from Italy by a British blockade, the lack of these essential resources led to a 20% fall in Italian steel production in 1940–42.

Italy soon faced mounting disasters. Attacks on France in 1940 were held off, and Mussolini gained nothing of significance from the eventual fall of France as Hitler did not want to antagonise the new Vichy government unnecessarily by allowing Italy to rob the French corpse. In September 1940 Italy invaded Libya and attacked British forces in Egypt, and then in October invaded Greece. Both invasions were thrown back, and in November 1940 British carrier-based aircraft sank half the Italian battle fleet at Taranto. Only German assistance saved Mussolini from defeat in North Africa and in Greece. By April 1941 the East African Empire, which had cost Mussolini the chance of working with Britain and France, had been lost.

Despite these disasters Mussolini gambled again when he supported Hitler in the 1941 invasion of the USSR, eventually sending 200,000 Italian troops to the Russian Front. Later that year he copied Hitler in declaring war on the USA, a mistake of astonishing proportions. By May 1943 North Africa had been lost, and in July the Allies invaded Sicily.

The fall of Mussolini and the Salo Republic, 1943–45

On the night of 24 July 1943, the Fascist Grand Council voted 19–7 to force Mussolini to resign. The conspiracy had been prompted by the string of Italian defeats and by the anger of leading Fascists Grandi and Bottai, who had been sacked in February 1943. Led by Farinacci and Emilio de Bono, these Fascists now tried to extricate themselves from the catastrophe of defeat. The war had broken the delicate balance of political forces that had sustained Mussolini. Both Fascists and the old elites now abandoned him. The king – showing a resolution notable for its absence since 1922 – became a rallying point for the growing opposition and dismissed Mussolini. Possessing no elite forces such as Hitler's SS, Mussolini could only accept the inevitable, namely the collapse of his dictatorship and the ignominy of imprisonment. As Denis Mack Smith has put it, "No regime in all history had fallen under such unanimous condemnation' (*Modern Italy, A Political History*, 1997). Mussolini was incarcerated in the mountain prison of Gran Casso. It appeared that his political career was over.

But the end was not yet nigh. In September 1943 Mussolini was rescued from captivity by the Germans, who still had a use for him. Backed by German force he set up a shrunken Fascist state in northern Italy. Often referred to as the Salo Republic, it was kept in existence by the Germans and totally dominated by them. Here the embittered Mussolini returned to his once rejected radical roots. The Verona Programme of November 1943 and the Socialization Law of February 1944 promised nationalisation, worker power, land reform and wage and price controls. The Duce had come full circle back to his socialist roots. However, the new radicalism was shunned by workers, ignored by capitalists and obstructed by the Germans. 'Fascism's attempt to redefine itself could not escape the taint of its past' (P. Morgan, *Italian Fascism*, 1995), and no new alliance with the workers was possible amidst the chaos of impending defeat. On 28 April 1945, while fleeing in disguise with retreating German

Figure 3
Map to show the main events and phases in Italian foreign policy, 1922–43

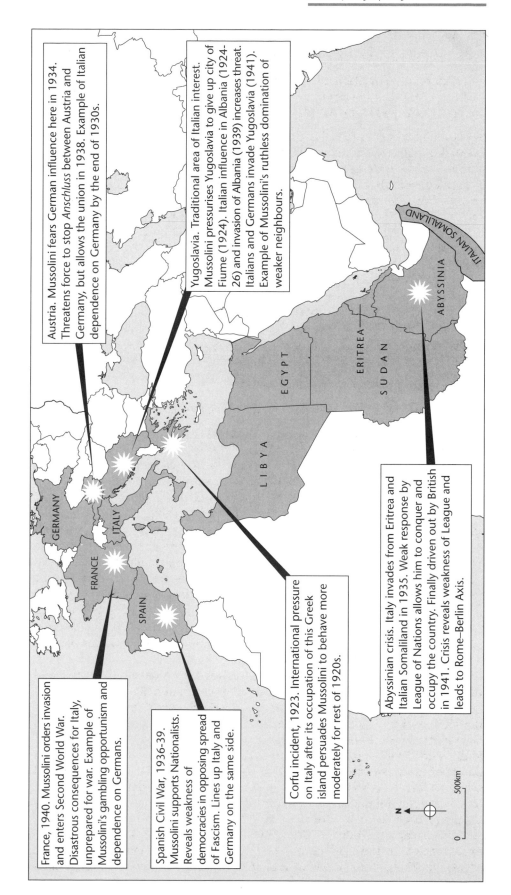

Austria. Mussolini fears German influence here in 1934. Threatens force to stop *Anschluss* between Austria and Germany, but allows the union in 1938. Example of Italian dependence on Germany by the end of 1930s.

Yugoslavia. Traditional area of Italian interest. Mussolini pressurises Yugoslavia to give up city of Fiume (1924). Italian influence in Albania (1924-26) and invasion of Albania (1939) increases threat. Italians and Germans invade Yugoslavia (1941). Example of Mussolini's ruthless domination of weaker neighbours.

France, 1940. Mussolini orders invasion and enters Second World War. Disastrous consequences for Italy, unprepared for war. Example of Mussolini's gambling opportunism and dependence on Germans.

Spanish Civil War, 1936-39. Mussolini supports Nationalists. Reveals weakness of democracies in opposing spread of Fascism. Lines up Italy and Germany on the same side.

Corfu incident, 1923. International pressure on Italy after its occupation of this Greek island persuades Mussolini to behave more moderately for rest of 1920s.

Abyssinian crisis. Italy invades from Eritrea and Italian Somaliland in 1935. Weak response by League of Nations allows him to conquer and occupy the country. Finally driven out by British in 1941. Crisis reveals weakness of League and leads to Rome–Berlin Axis.

troops, Mussolini was recognised by communist partisans and executed along with his mistress, Clara Petacci. Their bodies were soon to hang upside down from the roof of a petrol station in Milan.

Why did Italy lose the war?

◆ Inadequate preparations. In 1940 the Italian army amounted to three million men, not the 'eight million bayonets' promised by Mussolini. The nation also lacked the natural and economic resources necessary to win.

◆ Geographically too ambitious. Attempts to dominate the Balkans, the Mediterranean and North Africa as well as hold on to the East African Empire were totally beyond Italy's capabilities.

◆ Wildly unrealistic diplomacy. Declaring war on the USSR and the USA were severe errors. These were states with huge resources.

◆ Lack of a trustworthy ally. Germany never treated Italy as an equal. Given Mussolini's unreliable track record this is hardly surprising.

◆ Italian disillusionment. The German alliance was always unpopular, and defeats severed Mussolini from all his major bases of support.

Studying the foreign policy of Fascist Italy

1 'I want to make Italy great, respected and feared' (Mussolini).
From what you have read and from your wider research, to what extent did Italian foreign policy fulfill this aim of Mussolini's?

2 Which of the four Options on pages 41–43 do you feel best explains the nature of Italian foreign policy? Explain why it is the best assessment. You will need to:
◆ support it with carefully chosen and relevant evidence.
◆ consider the opinions of historians.
◆ explain why you think it is a more persuasive explanation than the other possible models.

6 Issues and interpretations

Key points

◆ Was Mussolini a modernising force in Italian history?
◆ To what extent does Mussolini represent a break in Italian tradition and history?
◆ The nature of Italian Fascism

Was Mussolini a modernising force in Italian history?

The nature of the debate

Official Fascist propaganda frequently claimed that Mussolini was transforming Italy into a modern industrial state. Today's historians are divided over the extent to which this was true. Within Italy the debate became particularly acute in 1994, the first year in which the extreme right in Italian politics had participated in government since 1945. This entry of the extreme right into a right-of-centre government led to much discussion over exactly what Mussolini's contribution to Italian history was and what he achieved.

Amongst modern Fascists, the model for analysing Mussolini's achievements has pivoted around the year 1938. It has been argued that before this date, he contributed a wide range of reforms which were responsible for a considerable degree of modernisation within Italy. After 1938, a process began which led to the disaster of the Second World War and the destruction of all that Fascism had achieved in its first sixteen years in power. This viewpoint is not confined to modern Fascists alone, as some more moderate Italian conservatives also find this interpretation attractive.

A number of historians have also called for a more open-minded appraisal of Mussolini's achievements and the direction of Fascist policy. Within Italy in the late 1980s, de Felice insisted that too many interpretations were influenced by the resistance movement which opposed Mussolini towards the end of the Second World War. Such approaches, he argued, ignored the popular support for Mussolini and simplified the complexity of his foreign policy.

A modernising force?

Denis Mack Smith has dismissed Mussolini as an incompetent, whose so-called achievements were nothing more than propaganda exercises without substance. Other historians have been less dismissive. De Felice identified a totalitarian 'potential' within the regime – a view which made less of the failures and concentrated more on the real power held by Mussolini.

A more extreme view has been advanced by A. James Gregor (*Italian Fascism and Developmental Dictatorship*, 1979). His study suggested that Fascism did achieve a coherent economic policy which led to a modern mixed economy, monetary discipline, and state intervention to stimulate modern industries. The Battle for Grain and the land reclamation schemes aided a move towards modern agriculture in a state where methods of farming were often backward. This interpretation suggests that there were significant achievements among the failures, and that the Fascist state had a predominantly modernising effect on Italian society and economics.

Other historians have rejected this viewpoint, most notably Paul Corner, Gustavo Corni and Vera Zamagni (*Economic History of Italy*, 1860–1990, 1993). The case against Mussolini as a successful moderniser has been summed up by Carl Levy (*From Fascism to Post Fascists* in R. Bessel (ed), *Fascist Italy and Nazi Germany, Comparison and Contrasts*, 1996). Levy has shown that money for land reclamation was poorly used, inappropriately expanding wheat production at the expense of citrus fruits. Despite its claims to the contrary, the Fascist regime failed to increase the number of small landowners, and many such landowners were reduced to leaseholders despite the government's supposed support for rural life. This failure to protect poor farmers led to an increased drift to urban areas. These are serious attacks on the modernising argument, since they suggest that not only did old-fashioned rural trends survive but that they actually became more deeply intrenched under Fascist influence. In rural areas, it was the landed rich who benefited at the expense of the poor.

Within industry, Levy has argued that the state involvement in the 1930s lacked real planning. Additionally, he has claimed that the nationalised industries were not really under state control, but instead managers were free to do as they wished. Industrial growth was mediocre, and less help was generally given to the economy than in the USA and in Britain. Mussolini and his government paid lip service to new production and management methods, but few such methods were actually implemented. The traditional industrial families still dominated industry, but under the overall control of the government.

In social terms the achievements were disappointing. The Fascist welfare state was primitive and chaotic, with no universal welfare provision. Instead, it was geared to specific occupations and did not replace those alternative schemes formerly supplied by socialist and Catholic trade unions. Fascist prejudice ensured that Italian society remained male-dominated, and the Dopolavoro largely benefited men. Pressures on women to combine both paid work and housework prevented their active participation in whatever Fascist education programmes were provided. Indeed, Fascist policies attempted to keep women in the home, which further supported traditional Italian society.

On balance it seems clear that where Mussolini did have a modernising influence it was often limited, poorly organised and overshadowed by the failure of Fascism to really change traditional Italy. Given the deep-rooted nature of Italian traditional society this is not wholly surprising.

To what extent does Mussolini represent a break in Italian tradition and history?

It is convenient to define Mussolini as making a break with Italian history. Such an interpretation was promoted by Fascists in the 1920s and 1930s who saw themselves as revolutionaries. The same ideas were later recycled by liberals who wished to disassociate the Italian Liberal state from Fascism.

This interpretation does not fit the overall pattern of events. Many of Mussolini's most distinctive policies were accelerations of existing trends. This is not to say that he did not influence the trends, merely to note that they did not originate with him and the PNF.

The territorial expansionism that was such a feature of the 1930s built on traditional trends in Italian foreign policy. Even the repressive nature of Fascism was assisted by previous government policies such as internal detention during the First World War and the political manipulation of local government prefects. Strangely enough, it was by using the authoritarian structure of the Liberal state that Mussolini was able to control the *squadristi* and their leaders. Even with regard to that most Fascist structure, the Corporate State, there were precedents. Pope Leo XIII (1878–1903) had sought to bring together workers and employers in mixed unions (corporations), which covered areas of economic activity. It was then suggested that these might form the basis for parliamentary representation.

Similarly, some Italian socialists (also known as syndicalists) had taken up the idea of corporations as a way by which working-class influence could be increased along with industrial output without resorting to class conflict (an approach called 'productivism'). As Martin Blinkhorn has put it, this apparently Fascist 'invention' was no such thing and 'its pedigree was long and complex' (M. Blinkhorn, *Mussolini and Fascist Italy*, 1984).

The nature of Italian Fascism

By the 1980s there had arisen four broad explanations of what caused Italian Fascism and contributed to its nature. These explanations have continued to develop but the main lines of argument are still discernible in later writings.

Explanation 1: Complex modern society

Fascism was the product of the increasingly complicated nature of society since the French Revolution. Linked to changes brought about by the Industrial Revolution, a situation was created which dissolved many traditional loyalties and structures. This left many people confused and rootless, hence Fascism's wide support in the 1920s and 1930s when it offered a new and united Italy. The evolution of such an interpretation was linked to writers such as Friedrich Meinecke and Gerhard Ritter.

Explanation 2: A temporary moral decay

The Italian historian Benedetto Croce identified Fascism as arising from a kind of moral decay which, though produced by long-term forces, was in itself temporary and a mere interruption in Italy's development as a liberal nation.

Unsophisticated masses were easily manipulated, and this manipulation was made easier by materialism, nationalism and the admiration for 'heroic' leaders. This ensured support despite reduced liberty.

Explanation 3: An underdeveloped state

This view held that Fascism arose from the historical weaknesses of particular states. In states which experienced slow economic development and late national independence, a small middle class sought an alliance with conservatives and anti-democratic groups in order to resist the working class and the the spread of communism. Italian Liberals failed to involve more people in the nation's affairs and, when broader democracy did arrive between 1912 and 1922, many people felt little loyalty towards the system of government. The evolution of this view was associated with historians E. Vermeil, Peter Viereck and Denis Mack Smith.

In Italy, the historian de Felice gave a particularly controversial twist to this interpretation by suggesting that Fascism was a revolutionary movement, powered by an emerging middle class keen to challenge traditional norms and controls. The eventual Fascist regime, de Felice argued, failed to realise these ambitions because of its compromises with the Italian elites. Consequently there were always tensions between Mussolini (keen to keep power) and the Fascist Party (keen to promote change).

Explanation 4: Capitalism in crisis

Marxist analysis suggested Fascism was the product of capitalist society in crisis. Faced with mounting working-class pressure for change and a collapse in economic stability, capitalists sought to harness popular unrest in order to present a veneer of change and reform which really masked the exploitation of the workers and the protection of the wealthy and powerful. Thus the Corporate State was merely a tool for exploitation. The evolution of this view was associated with Leon Trotsky, Richard Lowenthal, Antonio Gramsci and Palmiro Togliatti. The latter two Italian communists recognised this interpretation had its flaws, most notably the fact that there was mass support for Fascism, and the difficulty in explaining why capitalism should turn to Fascism when the Liberal state had previously defended its interests.

Studying issues and interpretations

1 From your own research, which of the interpretations of the nature of Italian Fascism do you find best explains the conduct of Mussolini's regime, 1922–45?

2 Devise a spider diagram to illustrate the case for and against Mussolini as a modernising force in Italian history. Which of these two interpretations do you think best fits the available evidence?

Structure of Italian government from December 1928

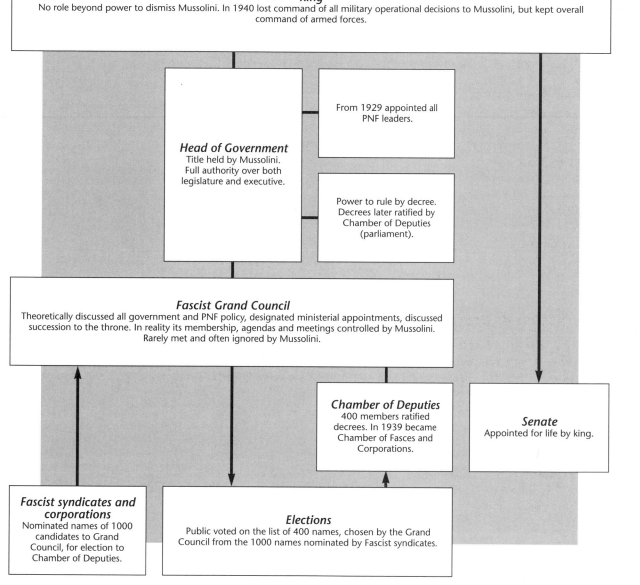

King
No role beyond power to dismiss Mussolini. In 1940 lost command of all military operational decisions to Mussolini, but kept overall command of armed forces.

Head of Government
Title held by Mussolini. Full authority over both legislature and executive.

From 1929 appointed all PNF leaders.

Power to rule by decree. Decrees later ratified by Chamber of Deputies (parliament).

Fascist Grand Council
Theoretically discussed all government and PNF policy, designated ministerial appointments, discussed succession to the throne. In reality its membership, agendas and meetings controlled by Mussolini. Rarely met and often ignored by Mussolini.

Chamber of Deputies
400 members ratified decrees. In 1939 became Chamber of Fasces and Corporations.

Senate
Appointed for life by king.

Fascist syndicates and corporations
Nominated names of 1000 candidates to Grand Council, for election to Chamber of Deputies.

Elections
Public voted on the list of 400 names, chosen by the Grand Council from the 1000 names nominated by Fascist syndicates.